I AM Proud of myself
SELF-ESTEEM

Name:

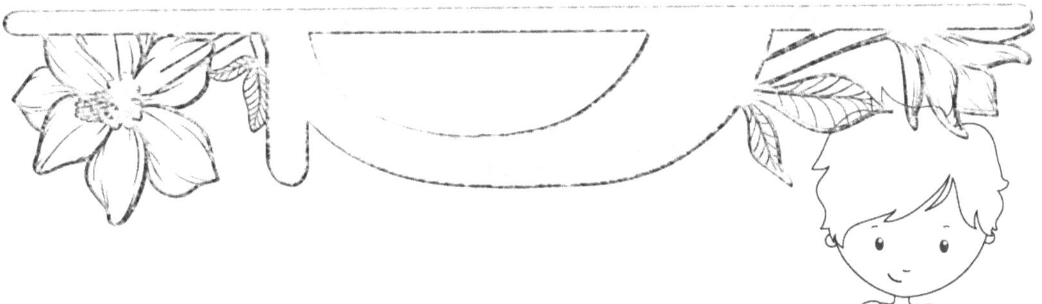

Copyright © 2023 Newbee Publication

ALL RIGHTS RESERVED

Thanks for Purchase
Scan QR code for more publications

This book may not be reproduced or transmitted in any form or by any means, electronic or mechanical, without written permission from the author.

I love myself just the way I am.

I love myself just the way I am.

I love myself just the way I am.

I love myself just the way I am.

I am prepared for new challenges.

I am prepared for new challenges.

I am prepared for new challenges.

I am worthy of the respect of others.

I am worthy of the respect of others.

I am worthy of the respect of others.

I am a valuable and important person.

I am a valuable and important person.

I am a valuable and important person.

I am a valuable and important person.

My potential is unlimited.

My potential is unlimited.

My potential is unlimited.

My potential is unlimited.

I believe in my abilities.

I believe in my abilities.

I believe in my abilities.

I believe in my abilities.

I deserve all that is good.

I deserve all that is good.

I deserve all that is good.

I deserve all that is good.

I deserve all that is good.

I deserve all that is good.

I am lovable.

I am lovable.

I am lovable.

I am lovable.

I am lovable.

A little step every day.

A little step every day.

A little step every day.

A little step every day.

A little step every day.

I am improving my capabilities.

I am improving my capabilities.

I am improving my capabilities.

I am improving my capabilities.

I am working on my challenges.

I am working on my challenges.

I am working on my challenges.

I am working on my challenges.

I will surely overcome my challenges.

I will surely overcome my challenges.

I will surely overcome my challenges.

I will surely overcome my challenges.

I will surely overcome my challenges.

I am capable and strong.

I am capable and strong.

I am capable and strong.

I am capable and strong.

I am capable and strong.

I am learning to love myself more.

I am learning to love myself more.

I am learning to love myself more.

I am learning to love myself more.

I am grateful for my life & who I am.

I am grateful for my life & who I am.

I am grateful for my life & who I am.

I accept myself just the way I am.

I accept myself just the way I am.

I accept myself just the way I am.

I have many good qualities.

I have many good qualities.

I have many good qualities.

I am worthy of my own love.

I am worthy of my own love.

I am worthy of my own love.

I am learning to trust myself & others.

I am learning to trust myself & others.

I am learning to trust myself & others.

I am in complete control of my life.

I am in complete control of my life.

I am in complete control of my life.

I am in complete control of my life.

I am learning to take care of myself.

I am learning to take care of myself.

I am learning to take care of myself.

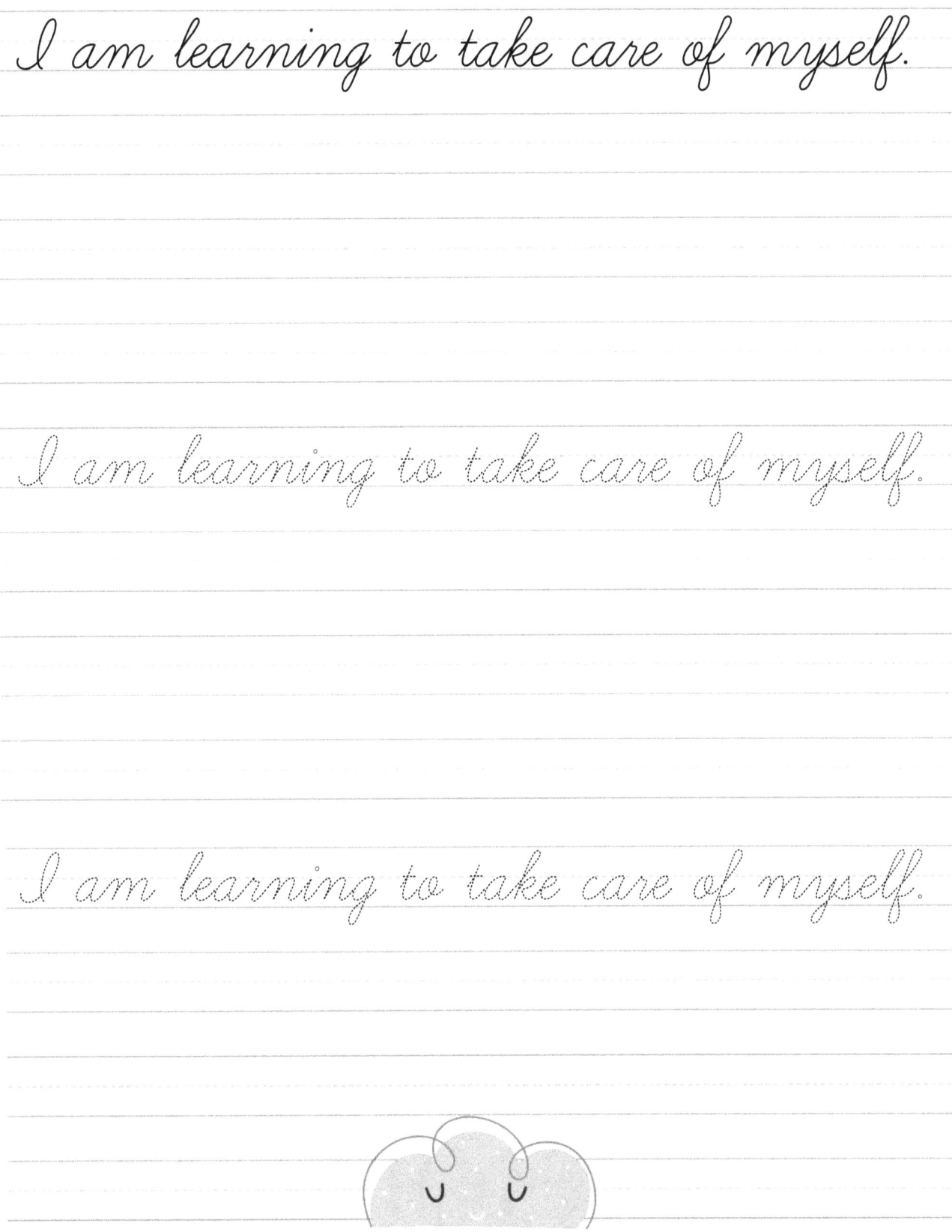

My feelings and needs are essential.

My feelings and needs are essential.

My feelings and needs are essential.

I am cheerful and optimistic.

I am cheerful and optimistic.

I am cheerful and optimistic.

I am cheerful and optimistic.

I am in charge of my emotions.

I am in charge of my emotions.

I am in charge of my emotions.

I am optimistic and excited about my life.

I am optimistic and excited about my life.

I believe in my ability to succeed.

I believe in my ability to succeed.

I believe in my ability to succeed.

I believe in my ability to succeed.

I am becoming healthier each day.

I am becoming healthier each day.

I am becoming healthier each day.

I am becoming healthier each day.

My determination is excellent.

My determination is excellent.

My determination is excellent.

My determination is excellent.

My determination is excellent.

I am doing the best I can.

I am doing the best I can.

I am doing the best I can.

I am doing the best I can.

I am at peace with myself.

I am at peace with myself.

I am at peace with myself.

I am at peace with myself.

I am becoming the best version of myself.

I am becoming the best version of myself.

I am becoming the best version of myself.

I attract positive people into my life.

I attract positive people into my life.

I attract positive people into my life.

I deserve to feel good about myself.

I deserve to feel good about myself.

I deserve to feel good about myself.

I deserve to feel good about myself.

I deserve to feel good about myself.

I am confident in learning new things.

I am confident in learning new things.

I am confident in learning new things.

I am learning to ask for help if needed.
I am learning to ask for help if needed.
I am learning to ask for help if needed.

I am learning to ask for help if needed.

I am talented, and I value my worth.

I am talented, and I value my worth.

I am talented, and I value my worth.

I am talented, and I value my worth.

I am talented, and I value my worth.

I am more confident each day.

I am more confident each day.

I am more confident each day.

I am more confident each day.

I am more confident each day.

I Create positive & supportive relationships.

I Create positive & supportive relationships.

I Create positive & supportive relationships.

I am right where I am supposed to be.

I am right where I am supposed to be.

I am right where I am supposed to be.

I am right where I am supposed to be.

I am a unique gift to the world.

I am a unique gift to the world.

I am a unique gift to the world.

I am a unique gift to the world.

I am a unique gift to the world.

I am a unique gift to the world.

I am resilient and can get through anything.

I am resilient and can get through anything.

I am resilient and can get through anything.

I am resilient and can get through anything.

I love myself unconditionally.

I love myself unconditionally.

I love myself unconditionally.

My growth is a continuous process.

My growth is a continuous process.

My growth is a continuous process.

My growth is a continuous process.

My growth is a continuous process.

I deserve to be happy.

I deserve to be happy.

I deserve to be happy.

I deserve to be happy.

I deserve to be happy.

I am learning to feel more confident in every situation.

I am learning to feel more confident in every situation.

I am learning to feel more confident in every situation.

I am learning to feel more confident in every situation.

I am living the life of my dreams.

I am living the life of my dreams.

I am living the life of my dreams.

I am living the life of my dreams.

I attract positive people into my life.

I attract positive people into my life.

I attract positive people into my life.

I attract positive people into my life.

I attract positive people into my life.

I will make good choices for myself.

I will make good choices for myself.

I will make good choices for myself.

I will make good choices for myself.

I will make good choices for myself.

I can keep my chin up when things are hard.

I can keep my chin up when things are hard.

I can keep my chin up when things are hard.

I can keep my chin up when things are hard.

I am loving and kind to myself.
I am loving and kind to myself.
I am loving and kind to myself.
I am loving and kind to myself.

I am loving and kind to myself.

I have flaws, and I don't have any complaints about them.

I have flaws, and I don't have any complaints about them.

I have flaws, and I don't have any complaints about them.

I am not afraid of failing.

I am not afraid of failing.

I am not afraid of failing.

I am not afraid of failing.

I am not afraid of failing.

I am not afraid of failing.

I am resilient and can face adversity.

I am resilient and can face adversity.

I am resilient and can face adversity.

I am resilient and can face adversity.

I am a valuable person to society.

I am a valuable person to society.

I am a valuable person to society.

I am a valuable person to society.

I can control my thoughts and feelings.

I can control my thoughts and feelings.

I can control my thoughts and feelings.

I can control my thoughts and feelings.

I can control my thoughts and feelings.

I am brave and have a positive mindset.

I am brave and have a positive mindset.

I am brave and have a positive mindset.

I am mindful of my actions.

I am mindful of my actions.

I am mindful of my actions.

I am mindful of my actions.

I am mindful of my actions.

I am mindful of my actions.

I am tough enough to handle challenges.

I am tough enough to handle challenges.

I am tough enough to handle challenges.

I am tough enough to handle challenges.

There are no limits to what I can do.

There are no limits to what I can do.

There are no limits to what I can do.

There are no limits to what I can do.

I control my thoughts and my body.
I control my thoughts and my body.
I control my thoughts and my body.

I control my thoughts and my body.

Every day my work makes me smarter.

Every day my work makes me smarter.

Every day my work makes me smarter.

Every day my work makes me smarter.

Pressure does not frighten me.

Pressure does not frighten me.

Pressure does not frighten me.

Pressure does not frighten me.

Pressure does not frighten me.

My life is full of opportunities.

My life is full of opportunities.

My life is full of opportunities.

My life is full of opportunities.

I acquire new knowledge and skills easily.

I am safe, and everything is okay.

I am safe, and everything is okay.

I am safe, and everything is okay.

I am safe, and everything is okay.

I am trying my best, and that is enough.

I am trying my best, and that is enough.

I am trying my best, and that is enough.

Everything is in my control.

Everything is in my control.

Everything is in my control.

Everything is in my control.

I have a strong body and mind.

I have a strong body and mind.

I have a strong body and mind.

I have a strong body and mind.

I can always find a way to achieve my goals.

I can always find a way to achieve my goals.

I can always find a way to achieve my goals.

My memory is better, and I trust my memory.

My memory is better, and I trust my memory.

My memory is better, and I trust my memory.

I strengthen my body and mind each day.

I strengthen my body and mind each day.

I strengthen my body and mind each day.

I strengthen my body and mind each day.

I have many talents, and I am learning to develop them.

I have many talents, and I am learning to develop them.

I have many talents, and I am learning to develop them.

Every challenge brings me new opportunities.

Every challenge brings me new opportunities.

Every challenge brings me new opportunities.

Every challenge brings me new opportunities.

I am optimistic about my life.

I am optimistic about my life.

I am optimistic about my life.

I am optimistic about my life.

I believe in myself more and more as
I grow and learn.

I believe in myself more and more as
I grow and learn.

I believe in myself more and more as
I grow and learn.

My positive attitude guarantees my success.

My positive attitude guarantees my success.

My positive attitude guarantees my success.

My potential is unlimited, and I believe in me.

My potential is unlimited, and I believe in me.

My potential is unlimited, and I believe in me.

I build myself up in every way.

I build myself up in every way.

I build myself up in every way.

I build myself up in every way.

I am much more intelligent than I think I am.

I am much more intelligent than I think I am.

I am much more intelligent than I think I am.

I enjoy problem-solving & learning opportunities.

I enjoy problem-solving & learning opportunities.

I enjoy problem-solving & learning opportunities.

I control my thoughts and my body.

I control my thoughts and my body.

I control my thoughts and my body.

I am cheerful and optimistic.

I am cheerful and optimistic.

I am cheerful and optimistic.

I have confidence in my ability to learn.

I have confidence in my ability to learn.

I have confidence in my ability to learn.

I have confidence in my ability to learn.

I have confidence in my ability to learn.

Mastering new knowledge makes me feel powerful.

Mastering new knowledge makes me feel powerful.

Mastering new knowledge makes me feel powerful.

There are no limits to what I can do and learn.

There are no limits to what I can do and learn.

There are no limits to what I can do and learn.

I am hardworking, and my efforts pay off.

I am hardworking, and my efforts pay off.

I am hardworking, and my efforts pay off.

I will succeed with patience and persistence.

I will succeed with patience and persistence.

I will succeed with patience and persistence.

Every day my work makes me smarter.

Every day my work makes me smarter.

Every day my work makes me smarter.

Every day my work makes me smarter.

Pressure does not frighten me.

Pressure does not frighten me.

Pressure does not frighten me.

Pressure does not frighten me.

I can overcome any obstacle.

I can overcome any obstacle.

I believe in my ability to succeed.

I control my thoughts and my body.

Everything is in my control.

I am learning to love myself more.

I am worthy of the respect of others.

My potential is unlimited.

Learning gives me faith in myself.

I am worthy of the respect of others.

I am larning to love myself more eachday.

I breathe in confidence and exhale fear.

I attract positive people into my life.

I am becoming the best version of myself.

I am talented, and I value my worth.

I am loving and kind to myself.

I am practising loving my life.

Each day is an opportunity and a gift.

I give myself the care and attention that I deserve.

I forgive myself & others and I allow myself to feel inner peace.

We would appreciate it if you could give a review on google
For More Publication visit our website

www.newbeepublication.com

www.ingramcontent.com/pod-product-compliance
Lightning Source LLC
Chambersburg PA
CBHW081710100526
44590CB00022B/3722